DevOps For Beginners...

MARK DAVIES

Copyright © 2024 Mark Davies

All rights reserved.

DEDICATION

To all the dedicated technical teams, in the many public and private sector businesses, I have been lucky enough to be a part of or to manage.

The journey is not to perfection but to efficiency, and if we can all do that more often and together then we will deliver more than it was ever thought possible.

CONTENTS

	Acknowledgments	i
1	Understanding DevOps: A Modern Approach to IT operations	3
2	Traditional I.T. Vs. DevOps: What's The Difference?	7
3	The Business Benefits of DevOps: Speed, Quality, And Cost Savings	11
4	Building The DevOps Culture: Collaboration, Communication, And Continuous Improvement	19
5	The DevOps Toolchain: Automation, Monitoring, And Continuous Delivery	27
6	Implementing DevOps in A Traditional I.T. Environment: Overcoming Common Challenges	39
7	Measuring Success: Key Metrics and KPIs For DevOps Performance	47
8	The Future of I.T. Operations: Scaling DevOps For Enterprise Growth	55

ACKNOWLEDGMENTS

I would like to acknowledge all the smarter people that have gone before me and are still going. They come up with new models, new technologies, new methods, new ways working from SCRUM to DevOps, from programming languages to networking protocols. They all add to the rich and exciting world that is IT and make businesses, and lives, better -most of the time!

From their work I have learnt, tried, developed, changed, and adapted, as we all do, in our own IT worlds. There is rarely one size fits all, though the principles are often the same. That is why it is important to continually learn and adapt to make your own IT world a better one for your business. If I can help with that in any small way, then reach out and let me know.

1
UNDERSTANDING DEVOPS: A MODERN APPROACH TO I.T. OPERATIONS

Introduction to DevOps

In today's fast-paced digital world, businesses face increasing pressure to deliver products and services more quickly, efficiently, and with fewer errors. Technology plays a central role in meeting these demands, and for many organizations, staying competitive means rethinking how IT or ICT and software development teams collaborate. This is where DevOps comes in.

DevOps, short for "Development and Operations," is more than just a set of tools or processes. It's a philosophy and a cultural shift that encourages closer collaboration between traditionally siloed teams—software developers and IT operations. The goal is simple but powerful: to deliver software and services faster, more reliably, and with higher quality.

Why DevOps Matters

Before we dive deeper into how DevOps works, let's explore why it matters, particularly for leaders and managers. At its core, DevOps addresses three critical pain points:

1. **Speed of Delivery**: In traditional IT environments, there are often long delays between development, testing, and deployment. DevOps aims to shorten this cycle by integrating these processes and enabling more frequent, incremental releases.
2. **Quality and Reliability**: By fostering collaboration between development and operations teams, DevOps promotes shared responsibility for software quality. Automated testing, monitoring, and feedback loops ensure that issues are detected and resolved early.
3. **Cost Efficiency:** DevOps reduces manual processes, duplication of effort, and downtime. This results in more efficient use of resources and ultimately lowers the overall cost of software delivery and maintenance.

The Evolution of IT Operations

To appreciate the significance of DevOps, it's helpful to understand the evolution of IT operations. In traditional models, the development and operations teams have often worked in isolation. Developers write code, then hand it off to operations teams to deploy and manage. This separation can lead to misunderstandings, delays, and inefficiencies, as the two groups may have different goals and incentives. Development teams typically focus on creating new features, while operations teams prioritize stability and uptime. The lack of alignment between these two objectives often results in friction, missed deadlines, and lower quality products.

DevOps emerged as a response to these challenges, aiming to break down the silos between development and operations. Instead of working in isolation, these teams collaborate throughout the entire software lifecycle, from planning and development to testing, deployment, and maintenance. This alignment creates a smoother, faster, and more reliable process, ensuring that businesses can deliver value to their customers more effectively.

Key Concepts in DevOps

To better understand DevOps, let's explore some key concepts:
1. **Collaboration**: DevOps encourages developers and operations teams to work together from the start of a project, sharing responsibilities and goals. This means that both teams are equally invested in the success of the software.
2. **Automation**: Automation is a fundamental component of DevOps. By automating repetitive tasks, such as testing, deployment, and infrastructure management, teams can focus on higher-level work. Automation also reduces the risk of human error and increases the speed of delivery.

3. **Continuous Integration and Continuous Delivery (CI/CD):** CI/CD is a practice that allows teams to integrate code into a shared repository frequently and automatically test and deploy it. This ensures that new features and bug fixes can be released to customers or the business quickly and reliably.
4. Monitoring and Feedback: DevOps promotes continuous monitoring of applications and infrastructure. This allows teams to detect and address issues before they become major problems, and to gather feedback that can inform future development.

Summary

DevOps represents a fundamental shift in how organizations approach software development and IT operations. By fostering collaboration, embracing automation, and prioritizing speed and quality, DevOps enables businesses to respond more quickly to market, customer or citizen demands and deliver greater value to the business as a whole. In the next chapter, we will explore how traditional IT operations models compare to DevOps and the limitations of a siloed approach.

2
TRADITIONAL IT VS. DEVOPS: WHAT'S THE DIFFERENCE?

In this chapter, we'll dive into the differences between traditional IT models and DevOps, and how these differences impact business outcomes. While traditional IT operations have worked for decades, they often create bottlenecks and delays that limit business agility. DevOps, in contrast, seeks to eliminate these barriers.

Traditional IT Operations: The Siloed Approach

In a traditional IT operations model, development, operations, and quality assurance teams operate independently. This "siloed" approach means that each team is responsible for a specific phase of the software lifecycle:

- **Development Team**: Focused on writing code and developing new features. Their primary concern is to ensure that new functionalities meet business requirements.
- **Operations Team**: Responsible for deploying and maintaining applications in production environments. They focus on stability, uptime, and ensuring that the infrastructure can handle production loads.
- **Quality Assurance Team (QA):** Positioned between development and operations, QA tests the software to ensure that it meets quality standards before it is released to customers. Many organizations do not have a formal QA team, and as such it is often not performed as well as it should and in some cases. Not at all!

The traditional model usually follows a waterfall or linear process, where each phase happens sequentially. For example, developers finish coding, then hand over the application to QA for testing, and only after testing is complete does the operations team deploy the application to production.

Challenges of Traditional IT Models

This sequential process has a number of inherent challenges, including:

1. **Long Lead Times**: Each phase is dependent on the completion of the previous one, which can lead to long wait times between development, testing, and deployment.
2. **Lack of Accountability**: Because teams work in silos, accountability is often fragmented. Developers may finish their work, but if something goes wrong in production, it's up to the operations team to fix it. This leads to a culture of blame rather than collaboration.
3. **Inflexibility**: Traditional models are not well-suited to today's fast-paced market demands. When customer needs or business priorities change, it can be difficult and time-consuming to adjust a project that is already in progress.
4. **Higher Risk of Failure**: Since testing and deployment happens late in the process, issues often go unnoticed until they reach production. Fixing problems at this stage is more difficult and costly.
5. **Lack of Clear View**: Developers being at the start of the process pipeline are sometimes not fully aware of all the uses (use cases) that the system will be put to and as such the end user will break the software because they ask it to do something it was never intended to do when the developer coded it!

The DevOps Approach: Breaking Down the Silos

DevOps seeks to eliminate these silos by fostering a collaborative environment where development, operations, and QA work together throughout the entire software lifecycle. Here's how:

1. **Collaboration from the Start:** In a DevOps model, all teams are involved from the planning phase through deployment. This ensures that everyone shares a common understanding of the project's goals and constraints.
2. **Shared Responsibility**: With DevOps, developers are more involved in the operational aspects of their applications. Similarly, operations teams participate in the development process, helping to shape how software is built and deployed. This shared responsibility reduces the "us versus them" mentality that often plagues traditional models. Often operations team will blame developers for 'throwing things over the fence', which typically means they don't believe it was properly developed, documented or handed over appropriately.
3. **Continuous Integration and Delivery (CI/CD):** Instead of waiting until the end of a project to test and deploy software, DevOps promotes continuous integration and delivery. This means that code is regularly integrated into a shared repository, automatically tested, and deployed in small increments. This reduces the risk of failure and allows teams to deliver new features faster.
4. **Automation**: A key aspect of DevOps is automating repetitive tasks such as testing, deployment, and infrastructure management. Automation reduces human error, increases efficiency, and allows teams to focus on higher-level tasks.

Summary

> In this chapter, we've explored the key differences between traditional IT operations and DevOps. While the traditional model operates in silos with sequential handoffs, DevOps emphasizes collaboration, shared responsibility, and automation. This results in faster, more reliable software delivery and a more adaptable organization.

3
THE BUSINESS BENEFITS OF DEVOPS: SPEED, QUALITY, AND COST SAVINGS

As organizations strive to stay competitive in an increasingly digital world and public sector authorities struggle with financial cuts, the benefits of DevOps become clear. It's not just about improving technical processes; DevOps has a direct impact on business outcomes. In this chapter, we'll explore how DevOps delivers tangible business value, including increased speed to market, higher product quality, and significant cost savings and greater customer and citizen value.

Faster Time to Market: Speed as a Competitive Advantage

One of the most immediate and compelling benefits of DevOps is the ability to deliver products and features more quickly. In traditional IT operations, long lead times are common due to the siloed nature of teams, manual processes, and the sequential workflow. This can result in months or even years between the conception of an idea and its delivery to customers.

This can be especially true in public sector where the IT team has to understand what are, in effect, multiple differing businesses in each of the various directorates serving citizen needs.

With DevOps, the emphasis on collaboration, automation, and continuous delivery drastically reduces the time it takes to bring a product or feature to market. Here's how:

1. **Continuous Integration (CI)**: CI ensures that developers frequently integrate their code into a shared repository. Automated testing is performed on each integration to catch issues early. This practice eliminates the bottleneck of waiting for a "code freeze" and subsequent long testing phases before deployment.
2. **Continuous Delivery (CD)**: In a DevOps environment, software is developed in small, manageable increments, which are automatically tested and deployed to production. This means that new features, bug fixes, and updates can be delivered to customers on a weekly, daily, or even hourly basis.

3. **Automated Deployment Pipelines**: DevOps leverages automated deployment pipelines that move code from development to production quickly and safely. This eliminates the need for manual intervention, reducing errors and speeding up delivery.

The business impact of faster time to market is significant. Organizations can respond more quickly to customer demands, capitalize on market opportunities, and stay ahead of competitors. In public sector this means faster to meet citizen needs and more able to consolidate or rationalize departments by integrating systems and processes. A faster feedback loop also enables businesses to test new ideas and iterate on them based on real customer feedback, leading to products and services that better meet customer needs and add greater business value.

Improved Quality and Reliability: Reducing Errors and Downtime

DevOps doesn't just accelerate delivery; it also improves the quality of the software and systems being delivered. By integrating testing and monitoring into every stage of the development and deployment process, DevOps minimizes the likelihood of bugs and operational issues making their way into production.

Here's how DevOps improves software and system quality:

1. **Automated Testing**: In traditional models, testing often happens at the end of the development cycle, which can lead to the discovery of issues too late in the process. DevOps embraces automated testing throughout development. Unit tests, integration tests, and user acceptance tests are run as part of the CI/CD pipeline, ensuring that code is thoroughly tested before it reaches production.
2. **Continuous Monitoring**: Once the software is deployed, DevOps practices include continuous

monitoring of applications and infrastructure. This ensures that performance issues, security vulnerabilities, and potential failures are detected early. Teams are able to act quickly to resolve these issues before they impact customers.
3. **Rollbacks and Quick Fixes**: Because changes are deployed incrementally, it's easier to identify and isolate issues. If something does go wrong, DevOps processes make it straightforward to roll back the change or deploy a fix rapidly.

Improved software quality results in fewer production issues, which means less downtime, higher reliability, and an overall better customer experience. For businesses, this translates to enhanced customer trust, fewer support costs, and a stronger market reputation. Less issues and downtime also has the advantage that staff are focussed on delivering more not fixing more!

Cost Efficiency: Doing More with Less

Another major benefit of adopting DevOps is cost savings. By streamlining processes, reducing manual tasks, and improving overall efficiency, organizations can deliver more value while reducing operational costs. Here are the keyways in which DevOps drives cost savings:

1. **Automation Reduces Manual Work**: Many tasks that were traditionally performed manually—such as testing, deployment, and infrastructure management—are automated in a DevOps environment. This reduces the amount of time teams spend on repetitive tasks, allowing them to focus on more valuable activities such as innovation and problem-solving.
2. **Efficient Resource Utilization**: DevOps enables organizations to use their IT resources more efficiently. For example, automated scaling and provisioning of cloud infrastructure allow businesses to dynamically

adjust their resource usage based on demand, reducing waste, and ensuring that they only pay for what they use.
3. **Reduced Downtime and Recovery Costs**: When issues arise in production, the cost of downtime can be substantial. For some organizations, even a few minutes of downtime can result in significant revenue loss. In public sector it downtime can impact the needs of the citizens or worse, affect their lives! By improving the reliability of software and reducing the time it takes to identify and resolve issues, DevOps minimizes downtime and the associated impacts and costs.
4. **Faster Feedback Loops**: With DevOps, the feedback loop between customers and development teams is shortened. This allows organizations to quickly identify what works and what doesn't, reducing the time and money spent on features that don't deliver value.

Enhancing Business Agility: Responding to Market Changes

In today's rapidly changing business environment, agility is essential. Organizations need to be able to pivot quickly, whether in response to shifting customer preferences, technological advancements, or competitive pressures or as in the case of public sector it can be dwindling finances and budget cuts. DevOps provides the flexibility needed to adapt in real-time.

1. **Faster Experimentation and Innovation**: DevOps enables teams to experiment with new features and technologies more easily. The ability to quickly build, test, and release software allows organizations to innovate faster and bring new products to market without the risk of long development cycles.
2. **Iterative Development**: Instead of delivering software in large, monolithic releases, DevOps encourages an iterative approach. Small, frequent releases allow organizations to continuously improve their products

based on customer feedback, leading to better alignment with market needs.
3. **Cross-Functional Collaboration**: DevOps fosters a culture of collaboration across departments. By breaking down silos between development, operations, and business teams, organizations can more effectively respond to market changes, align on business objectives, and deliver products that meet customer expectations.

Customer Satisfaction: Delivering Better Experiences

Ultimately, the benefits of DevOps extend beyond the organization itself; they have a direct impact on customers and citizen's. By delivering high-quality software quickly and reliably, businesses can provide a better customer experience.

1. **Frequent Updates and Features**: DevOps enables companies to release new features and updates more frequently. This keeps customers engaged and ensures that their needs are continuously being met.
2. **Increased Reliability**: Fewer bugs, less downtime, and more reliable services lead to happier customers. Reliability is crucial in today's digital world, where customers can expect services to be available 24/7.
3. **Faster Response to Feedback**: With shorter development cycles and frequent releases, businesses can respond to customer feedback more quickly. This results in products that are better tailored to customer needs, driving higher satisfaction and loyalty.

Summary

In this chapter, we've examined the business benefits of adopting DevOps. The ability to deliver products and services faster, with higher quality, and at a lower cost has a profound impact on an organization's competitiveness, customer satisfaction and ability to meet citizen's needs. By embracing automation, collaboration, and continuous improvement, organizations can unlock new levels of efficiency and agility. In the next chapter, we'll explore how building the right DevOps culture is critical to realizing these benefits and sustaining long-term success.

4
BUILDING THE DEVOPS CULTURE: COLLABORATION, COMMUNICATION, AND CONTINUOUS IMPROVEMENT

Adopting DevOps is not just about implementing new tools or processes; it's about creating a culture that fosters collaboration, communication, and continuous improvement. A successful DevOps transformation requires a shift in mindset, where development, operations, and business teams work together toward common goals. In this chapter, we'll explore what a DevOps culture looks like, why it's important, and how organizations can foster this culture to maximize the benefits of DevOps.

The Importance of Culture in DevOps

When organizations attempt to implement DevOps without addressing cultural change, they often struggle to achieve meaningful results. This is because DevOps, at its core, is a philosophy that prioritizes collaboration and shared ownership. Without a cultural shift, the traditional silos between development and operations will persist, and the potential benefits of DevOps—speed, quality, and efficiency—will remain out of reach. The change must be predicated on the People, Process, Tools (technology) model and in that order.

DevOps culture is built on a few key principles:

1. **Collaboration**: DevOps aims to break down the silos between development, operations, and other teams like QA, security, and even business functions. These teams should no longer work in isolation but collaborate continuously throughout the software development lifecycle. This shared responsibility for both development and operations helps align the goals of different teams and promotes better communication.
2. **Communication**: Effective communication is the foundation of DevOps. It ensures that everyone involved in the software delivery process—developers, operations, product owners, and other stakeholders—are aligned on objectives, timelines, and constraints. Open and frequent communication reduces misunderstandings

and improves decision-making. (Many organizations struggle with decision making)
3. **Continuous Improvement**: DevOps culture emphasizes learning and improvement. By fostering a mindset of continuous improvement, teams are encouraged to experiment, fail fast, learn from mistakes, and iterate quickly. This focus on continuous improvement leads to better processes, higher quality products, and more efficient workflows. But it does require management to accept and understand mistakes are part of the process!

Fostering a Collaborative Environment

One of the primary goals of DevOps is to create a collaborative environment where development and operations teams work together as a unified group. In a traditional IT model, developers focus on writing code, and operations teams are responsible for deploying and maintaining that code in production. These separate responsibilities can create friction, as the teams may have conflicting priorities—developers want to release new features quickly, while operations teams want to ensure system stability.

To foster collaboration, organizations must encourage teams to share responsibilities and work toward a common goal. Here's how:

1. **Cross-Functional Teams**: One of the best ways to encourage collaboration is to organize teams around products or services rather than functions. Cross-functional teams, which include members from development, operations, and other areas such as QA, security, and product management, ensure that all relevant expertise is available throughout the project lifecycle. This promotes shared ownership and accountability.
2. **Shared Goals and Metrics**: DevOps encourages teams to work toward common business objectives rather than

individual team goals. For example, instead of measuring developers by the number of features they deliver and operations by uptime alone, both teams should be measured by their ability to deliver features quickly while maintaining stability. By aligning on shared goals and metrics, teams are incentivized to work together to achieve the best outcomes for the organization.
3. **DevOps Champions**: In many organizations, cultural change starts with leadership. Appointing DevOps champions—individuals or teams who advocate for and lead the DevOps transformation—can help drive the adoption of new practices. These champions can mentor other teams, demonstrate the benefits of collaboration, and address resistance to change.
4. **Finger pointing and blame must go**! No one, not even managers (or CEO's) can or should blame teams or individuals. The smoothest moves to DevOps come when a nurturing, accepting and most of all, SAFE, environment is created.

Communication: Breaking Down Silos

Effective communication is a cornerstone of any successful DevOps implementation. In traditional IT environments, communication between development and operations teams is often limited to hand-offs at specific stages of the project. This can lead to misunderstandings, delays, and a lack of visibility into the overall progress of the project.

DevOps requires a more integrated approach to communication, where teams continuously share information and feedback. Here are some strategies to improve communication in a DevOps environment:

1. **Regular Stand-ups and Meetings**: Daily stand-ups or short status meetings are a common practice in DevOps teams. These meetings provide an opportunity for team members to share updates, discuss challenges, and

coordinate their efforts. This ensures that everyone is on the same page and that issues are addressed quickly.
2. **Shared Tools and Platforms**: DevOps teams often use shared collaboration tools that enable real-time communication and visibility into the software development lifecycle. Tools like Slack, Microsoft Teams, or Jira allow teams to collaborate more effectively, track progress, and resolve issues in real time. These tools break down the communication barriers that typically exist between development and operations.
3. **Blameless Post-Mortems**: In a DevOps culture, failures are viewed as learning opportunities rather than reasons for blame. When an incident occurs, teams conduct blameless post-mortems to analyze what went wrong and how to prevent similar issues in the future. This open, transparent approach to communication fosters trust and continuous improvement.
4. **Be Blameless Everywhere**: The blameless approach must be fully adopted. Too often people pay lip service to the approach and show no blame in a stand-up but later moan about someone in the break room. It must be accepted, and no blame shown or felt.

Encouraging Continuous Improvement

DevOps is built on the principle of continuous improvement. This means that teams are always looking for ways to enhance their processes, reduce waste, and deliver better products more efficiently. A key part of this mindset is recognizing that perfection is not the goal—learning and adapting quickly is.

Here are some ways to foster a culture of continuous improvement:

1. **Embrace Experimentation**: DevOps teams are encouraged to experiment with new technologies, tools, and practices. This may include testing new automation tools, trying out different deployment strategies, or

experimenting with infrastructure as code. By creating a safe environment for experimentation, teams can find innovative ways to improve efficiency and effectiveness.
2. **Iterative Development**: Rather than waiting for a perfect solution, DevOps teams focus on delivering small, incremental improvements. This iterative approach allows teams to release features and updates more frequently, gather feedback from users, and adjust based on that feedback.
3. **Regular Retrospectives**: Retrospectives are meetings held at regular intervals (e.g., at the end of each sprint – development cycle) where teams reflect on what went well, what didn't, and how they can improve moving forward. Retrospectives are a key part of the continuous improvement process, allowing teams to learn from their experiences and make adjustments that lead to better outcomes.

Leadership's Role in Shaping DevOps Culture

Leaders play a critical role in shaping the DevOps culture within an organization. Without support from leadership, it's difficult to drive the cultural change required to make DevOps successful. Leaders must model the behaviour they expect from their teams and create an environment that supports collaboration, communication, and continuous improvement.

Here are some ways leaders can foster a DevOps culture:

1. **Promote Collaboration**: Leaders should encourage collaboration across departments and eliminate the barriers that prevent teams from working together. This may involve restructuring teams, providing shared tools, or incentivizing cross-functional collaboration.
2. **Empower Teams**: DevOps teams need the autonomy to make decisions and implement changes quickly. Leaders should empower teams to take ownership of their work and trust them to make the right decisions.

This means providing the tools, resources, and authority necessary to implement DevOps practices effectively.
3. **Reward Continuous Improvement**: Leaders should recognize and reward teams that embrace continuous improvement. This could involve celebrating successes, providing opportunities for professional development, or offering incentives for teams that demonstrate a commitment to innovation and efficiency.
4. If department directors are not working together and become defensive and parochial then this will not work. The DevOps approach is for the good of the organisation and not one individual directorate or department. Therefore, the leader at the top must buy in to the changes needed and work to ensure behaviours match need. This is often where failures occur.

Overcoming Resistance to Change

It's common for organizations to encounter resistance when attempting to implement a DevOps culture. This resistance may come from individuals or teams who are comfortable with the status quo or who fear that new processes will disrupt their workflows. Overcoming resistance to change is a key part of a successful DevOps transformation.

Here are some strategies to overcome resistance:

1. Communicate the Benefits: It's important to communicate the "why" behind the DevOps transformation. When teams understand how DevOps will improve their work, reduce manual tasks, and lead to better outcomes for the organization, they are more likely to embrace change.
2. Provide Training and Support: Adopting new tools and processes can be challenging, especially for teams that are used to working in a specific way. Providing training, resources, and ongoing support can help ease the transition and build confidence in the new approach.

3. Start Small and Scale: Rather than trying to implement DevOps across the entire organization at once, start with a small team or project. Demonstrating success on a small scale can build momentum and help overcome resistance in other parts of the organization.

Summary

> A successful DevOps implementation depends on building the right culture—one that emphasizes collaboration, communication, and continuous improvement. By fostering cross-functional teams, improving communication, and encouraging a mindset of continuous learning, organizations can unlock the full potential of DevOps. And of course, all in a safe no-blame culture. In the next chapter, we will explore the DevOps toolchain, focusing on the key tools and technologies that enable DevOps practices

5
THE DEVOPS TOOLCHAIN: AUTOMATION, MONITORING, AND CONTINUOUS DELIVERY

While DevOps is fundamentally a cultural and philosophical shift, tools and technologies play a critical role in enabling the practices that make DevOps successful. Automation, monitoring, and continuous delivery are essential components of the DevOps toolchain, and they help organizations achieve the speed, efficiency, and quality that DevOps promises. In this chapter, we will explore the key tools and technologies used in DevOps, how they fit together, and how they can help your organization streamline workflows and improve outcomes.

The Role of Tools in DevOps

DevOps tools are designed to automate and streamline the tasks involved in developing, testing, deploying, and monitoring software. These tools reduce the time it takes to move from code to production, ensure consistency, and minimize human error. Importantly, the tools are not a substitute for collaboration or cultural change, but they are critical enablers of the processes and workflows that DevOps fosters.

There are many tools available that support different aspects of the DevOps lifecycle, and each organization can choose the ones that best fit their needs. However, no tool can replace the need for shared responsibility and collaboration between teams. The best DevOps tools are those that integrate well across the development and operations teams, providing transparency and communication throughout the process.

Automation: The Heart of the DevOps Toolchain

Automation is at the core of DevOps, as it enables organizations to achieve faster, more reliable deployments while reducing manual effort. Automating repetitive and time-consuming tasks allows teams to focus on higher-value activities, such as innovation and problem-solving.

Some key areas where automation plays a critical role in DevOps include:

1. **Continuous Integration (CI)** Continuous integration involves the frequent merging of code into a shared repository, where it is automatically tested and validated. The goal is to catch issues early and prevent integration problems from snowballing into larger issues.
   Automation tools for continuous integration handle the following:

   - Code Integration: Automating the process of merging code from different developers into the main branch ensures that integration is seamless and conflicts are resolved early.
   - Automated Testing: Once code is integrated, automated tests (such as unit tests, integration tests, and end-to-end tests) are run to ensure that the code works as expected and doesn't introduce new bugs.

   Popular CI tools include Jenkins, CircleCI, Travis CI, and GitLab CI/CD. These tools help teams build, test, and validate code quickly and efficiently.

2. **Continuous Delivery (CD)** Continuous delivery is the process of automatically deploying code to production or staging environments once it has passed all automated tests. This allows teams to release new features and updates more frequently, with confidence that they won't break existing functionality. CD tools help automate:

   - Deployment: Automating the process of moving code from development to production environments ensures that deployments are consistent and reliable.
   - Infrastructure as Code (IaC): Managing infrastructure through code allows teams to automate the provisioning, configuration, and scaling of infrastructure. Tools like Terraform,

Ansible, and AWS CloudFormation enable teams to treat infrastructure as a versioned, repeatable artifact, ensuring consistency across environments.

By automating both the testing and deployment phases, teams can reduce the risk of human error, speed up the release process, and increase overall reliability.

3. **Configuration Management** Configuration management tools ensure that the software and infrastructure environments are configured consistently. These tools automate the process of managing and applying configurations to servers, databases, networks, and other infrastructure components. This guarantees that all environments—from development to production—are identical, reducing the likelihood of configuration drift and unexpected issues in production.

    It is not uncommon for teams to use test environments that are *nothing* like production and then wonder why systems fail when software is released. Configuration management removes that issue.

    Some popular configuration management tools in DevOps include Ansible, Puppet, Chef, and SaltStack. These tools provide the ability to automate the provisioning and management of infrastructure, making deployments smoother and more reliable.

4. **Continuous Testing** Testing automation is a critical component of the DevOps pipeline. Automated tests validate that the code behaves as expected at each stage of the development process. This includes:

- Unit Testing: Testing individual components of the codebase to ensure they function as intended.
- Integration Testing: Testing how different components of the system interact with each other.
- End-to-End Testing: Simulating user interactions with the application to ensure that the overall system behaves as expected.

Tools like Selenium, JUnit, TestNG, and Postman are commonly used to automate these testing processes, ensuring rapid feedback and continuous validation of the code.

Monitoring: Ensuring Reliability and Performance

In a DevOps environment, continuous monitoring is essential for ensuring that applications and infrastructure perform as expected in production. Monitoring provides teams with real-time visibility into system performance, security, and availability, enabling them to detect issues early and respond proactively.

Key aspects of monitoring in DevOps include:

1. **Infrastructure Monitoring** Monitoring the health and performance of infrastructure (such as servers, databases, and network components) ensures that any potential issues are identified before they impact the user experience. This includes tracking CPU usage, memory consumption, disk space, and network throughput.

    - Tools like Prometheus, Nagios, Datadog, and Grafana provide infrastructure monitoring and alerting, helping teams respond quickly to any deviations from normal operation.

2. **Application Performance Monitoring (APM)** Monitoring the performance of applications in production is critical to ensuring a positive user experience. APM tools provide insights into how well the application is performing under real-world conditions, including response times, error rates, and transaction volumes.

   - Tools like New Relic, AppDynamics, and Dynatrace help teams monitor application performance, diagnose issues, and optimize the user experience.

3. **Log Management and Analysis** Logs are a valuable source of information for diagnosing and resolving issues. Log management tools aggregate logs from different parts of the system (servers, applications, containers, etc.) and provide search, analysis, and alerting capabilities.

   - Tools like Splunk, ELK Stack (Elasticsearch, Logstash, and Kibana), and Graylog allow teams to monitor logs in real time, detect anomalies, and quickly resolve incidents.

4. **Security Monitoring** Security is a critical aspect of any DevOps toolchain, and monitoring for security threats is a continuous effort. DevOps teams can integrate security monitoring tools into the CI/CD pipeline to automatically detect vulnerabilities in the code, infrastructure, or dependencies. This proactive approach, often called "*DevSecOps*," ensures that security is baked into every stage of the process, rather than being an afterthought.

- Tools like Aqua, Twistlock, and Snyk are used to scan code, containers, and infrastructure for security vulnerabilities in real time.

Continuous Delivery: Ensuring Seamless Releases

Continuous delivery (CD) is the practice of automatically deploying code changes to production environments once they have been tested and validated. The goal is to ensure that new features, bug fixes, and updates are delivered to the business or customers as quickly as possible, without introducing risks.

Key elements of continuous delivery include:

1. Version Control and Branching Version control is essential for tracking changes to the codebase and enabling collaboration between developers. In a DevOps environment, it's common to use a "trunk-based" development approach, where code is continuously merged into a single main branch, and feature branches are short-lived.

    - Git is the most popular version control system used in DevOps, and it integrates with many CI/CD tools to automate the build, testing, and deployment process.

2. **Blue-Green Deployments** Blue-green deployments are a technique that ensures zero downtime during releases by maintaining two identical production environments. One environment (blue) serves live traffic, while the other (green) is used to deploy and test the new code. Once the new version is verified, traffic is switched to the green environment.

- Tools like Kubernetes and AWS Elastic Beanstalk facilitate blue-green deployments, enabling seamless updates and rollbacks.

3. **Canary Releases** In a canary release, new features are rolled out to a small subset of users before being fully deployed to the entire user base. This allows teams to gather feedback and verify the stability of the new version before a full rollout. If any issues are detected, the deployment can be rolled back with minimal impact.

    - CI/CD tools can be configured to support canary releases by automatically directing a portion of traffic to the new version while monitoring its performance.

4. **Rollback Strategies** In the event that a deployment introduces issues, having an automated rollback strategy is essential to minimizing downtime and impact on users. Many DevOps tools provide built-in mechanisms for rolling back changes in a controlled and automated manner.

    - Tools like Jenkins, GitLab, and Azure DevOps support rollback mechanisms, allowing teams to revert to a previous stable version of the application with minimal disruption.

The DevOps Toolchain in Action

The most effective DevOps toolchain is one that integrates multiple tools into a seamless, automated pipeline that covers the entire software development lifecycle—from coding and testing to deployment and monitoring. Here's an example of how a typical DevOps toolchain might look:

1. Version Control (Git): Developers push code to a shared repository.
2. Continuous Integration (Jenkins): The code is automatically built and tested using automated CI tools.
3. Infrastructure as Code (Terraform): Infrastructure is provisioned and configured automatically.
4. Continuous Delivery (GitLab CI/CD): Once tests pass, the code is deployed to production using automated deployment pipelines.
5. Monitoring (Prometheus, Grafana): Real-time monitoring tools track the performance and health of the system in production.
6. Log Management (ELK Stack): Logs are aggregated and analyzed for insights and troubleshooting.
7. Security Monitoring (Aqua): Continuous security scanning ensures that vulnerabilities are identified and addressed as early as possible in the pipeline, preventing potential security breaches or vulnerabilities from reaching production environments.

Selecting the Right Tools for Your Organization

Selecting the right tools for your DevOps toolchain is not a one-size-fits-all process. Every organization has unique needs, constraints, and goals, not least of all the cost and time to learn to use them, and the tools you choose should reflect those factors. Here are a few guidelines to consider when selecting DevOps tools:

1. **Integration and Compatibility**: One of the key considerations when choosing DevOps tools is their ability to integrate seamlessly with other tools in the pipeline. Look for tools that offer robust APIs, webhooks, and plugins to ensure that all stages of the development lifecycle are connected. For example, your CI tool should integrate smoothly with your version control system, testing framework, and deployment platform.

2. **Ease of Use and Adoption**: A tool that's difficult to use or requires significant training can slow down adoption and reduce productivity. Ensure that the tools you select are user-friendly and come with clear documentation, strong community support, and training resources.
3. **Scalability**: As your organization grows, your DevOps tools must be able to scale along with it. Consider whether the tools you choose can handle increasing volumes of code, infrastructure, and traffic without performance degradation. For example, container orchestration tools like Kubernetes are built to scale dynamically based on demand, making them ideal for larger organizations.
4. **Cost**: While many DevOps tools offer free tiers or open-source versions, costs can quickly add up as your organization grows. Be sure to factor in the cost of licenses, hosting, and support when selecting tools for your DevOps pipeline. Evaluate whether a paid tool offers enough value and ROI compared to its free or open-source alternatives.
5. **Security and Compliance**: In industries where security and regulatory compliance are critical, it's important to choose DevOps tools that provide strong security features. This includes the ability to enforce security policies, conduct vulnerability scanning, and provide audit logs for compliance purposes.
6. **Automation Capabilities**: The core of any DevOps toolchain is automation. The tools you select should enable automation for testing, deployment, monitoring, and infrastructure management. Evaluate whether a tool provides out-of-the-box automation or requires significant customization to achieve your goals.

The Future of the DevOps Toolchain

The DevOps toolchain is continually evolving, with new tools and practices emerging to meet the demands of modern software development. As organizations increasingly move to cloud-native architectures, containerization, and microservices, the tools that enable DevOps will continue to adapt.

1. **Cloud-Native DevOps**: As more organizations adopt cloud infrastructure, tools that are cloud-native—built specifically for cloud environments—are becoming more prominent. Kubernetes, Docker, and serverless platforms like AWS Lambda are transforming how organizations deploy and manage their applications in the cloud. Cloud-native DevOps tools are designed to take full advantage of the scalability, flexibility, and automation capabilities of cloud platforms.
2. **AI and Machine Learning in DevOps**: The integration of AI and machine learning into DevOps practices is a growing trend. These technologies can be used to optimize the performance of applications, predict, and prevent incidents, and automate decision-making processes. For example, AI-driven anomaly detection tools can monitor infrastructure and application performance to identify potential issues before they become critical.
3. **DevSecOps**: As security becomes an increasingly critical concern, DevOps practices are evolving into DevSecOps—an approach that integrates security into every stage of the development and deployment process. Tools that automate security testing, vulnerability scanning, and compliance checks will continue to be essential components of the modern DevOps toolchain.
4. **GitOps**: GitOps is an emerging practice that extends DevOps principles to infrastructure management by using Git as the source of truth for infrastructure configuration. With GitOps, all infrastructure changes are made through Git pull requests, and automation tools like Terraform or Kubernetes apply these changes automatically. This approach simplifies infrastructure management and provides a clear audit trail of changes.

Summary

In this chapter, we've explored the key components of the DevOps toolchain, including automation, continuous integration, continuous delivery, monitoring, and security. The tools that make up the DevOps toolchain are essential enablers of the cultural and process changes that DevOps requires. By automating repetitive tasks, providing real-time visibility into system performance, and ensuring reliable deployments, these tools allow organizations to achieve the speed, quality, and efficiency that DevOps promises.

However, selecting the right tools is only part of the equation. The true value of DevOps comes from integrating these tools into a cohesive pipeline that aligns with your organization's goals and fosters collaboration between development and operations teams. IT is also important that different teams do not use different tools to perform the same task, unfortunately everyone has favourites so this can happen more often than one would like!

In the next chapter, we'll discuss how to implement DevOps in a traditional IT environment, including overcoming the common challenges that organizations face when transitioning from a siloed model to a DevOps approach.

6
IMPLEMENTING DEVOPS IN A TRADITIONAL I.T. ENVIRONMENT: OVERCOMING COMMON CHALLENGES

Transitioning from a traditional IT operations model to a DevOps approach can be a challenging process, especially for organizations that have deeply ingrained workflows and legacy systems. However, the benefits of adopting DevOps—faster time to market, improved product quality, and greater efficiency—make the effort worthwhile. In this chapter, we will explore the common challenges organizations face when implementing DevOps in a traditional IT environment and provide practical strategies to overcome these obstacles.

The Challenge of Breaking Down Silos

In traditional IT environments, teams are often siloed, with developers, operations, quality assurance (QA), and security teams working independently of one another. Each team typically has its own goals, processes, and tools, which can lead to misalignment and inefficiency. Developers focus on delivering new features, while operations teams prioritize system stability and uptime. This separation often results in delays, friction, and finger-pointing when issues arise.

Overcoming the Silo Challenge

1. **Promote Cross-Functional Collaboration**: The first step in breaking down silos is to promote collaboration between development, operations, QA, and other teams. One way to achieve this is by forming cross-functional teams that include representatives from each area. These teams should be responsible for the entire software development lifecycle, from design and development to testing, deployment, and maintenance. By working together as a unified team, everyone shares the same goals and priorities.
2. **Foster a Culture of Shared Responsibility**: In a DevOps environment, everyone involved in the software development process is responsible for both the code and the infrastructure it runs on. This means developers are more involved in operations, and operations teams

participate earlier in the development process. Fostering a culture of shared responsibility ensures that both teams are aligned in their objectives and can collaborate more effectively to achieve the same business outcomes.
3. **Adopt Collaborative Tools**: Tools that enable real-time collaboration, such as chat platforms (Slack, Microsoft Teams), project management software (Jira, Trello), and integrated development environments (GitHub, GitLab), can help bridge the communication gap between siloed teams. These tools create a centralized platform where team members can share updates, raise issues, and track progress.

Legacy Systems and Infrastructure: A Barrier to DevOps

Many organizations still rely on legacy systems and infrastructure that were not designed for the level of agility and automation required by DevOps. Legacy systems often have complex dependencies, are difficult to integrate with modern DevOps tools, and can be prone to outages during deployment. Additionally, manual processes associated with maintaining legacy systems can slow down the delivery pipeline. This can be especially true in public sector where the large monolithic app is king. Each department has its own line of business system often using old technology, limited integration and almost zero data sharing capabilities.

Overcoming the Legacy Systems Challenge

1. **Incremental Modernization**: A complete overhaul of legacy systems is often unrealistic, especially for large enterprises. Instead, organizations should aim for incremental modernization. This could involve breaking down monolithic applications into smaller, more manageable microservices, or adopting cloud infrastructure for new projects while maintaining legacy systems for existing services. By modernizing

incrementally, organizations can reduce risk and gradually introduce DevOps practices.
2. **Containerization**: One of the key benefits of containerization (using tools like Docker) is that it allows legacy applications to be packaged with all their dependencies into isolated, portable containers. This means that legacy applications can run consistently across different environments—whether on-premises or in the cloud—without being affected by underlying infrastructure changes. Containers also make it easier to automate testing, deployment, and scaling.
3. **Infrastructure as Code (IaC)**: For organizations with legacy infrastructure, adopting Infrastructure as Code (IaC) practices can be a game changer. IaC tools like Terraform, AWS CloudFormation, and Ansible allow teams to define and manage infrastructure using code. This enables organizations to automate the provisioning and configuration of infrastructure, reducing manual effort and improving consistency across environments.

Resistance to Change: People and Processes

One of the biggest obstacles to implementing DevOps is resistance to change. This resistance can come from all levels of the organization—whether it's developers who are comfortable with their existing processes, operations teams who fear losing control over production environments, or senior management who are hesitant to invest in new tools and training. Overcoming this resistance requires a combination of leadership, education, and clear communication.

Overcoming Resistance to Change

1. **Leadership Buy-In**: Successful DevOps implementations require strong leadership support. Leaders must communicate the benefits of DevOps clearly and align the transformation with the organization's broader business goals. Without

leadership buy-in, it's difficult to secure the necessary resources and overcome resistance from teams who are reluctant to change.
2. **Start Small and Scale Gradually**: Rather than attempting to implement DevOps across the entire organization in one go, it's often more effective to start with a small pilot project. By selecting a single team or project to adopt DevOps practices, organizations can demonstrate the value of DevOps on a smaller scale. Once the pilot project is successful, the lessons learned can be applied to other teams, and DevOps practices can gradually scale across the organization.
3. **Invest in Training and Education**: Many organizations underestimate the importance of training when adopting DevOps. Teams need to be equipped with the skills and knowledge required to use new tools, automate processes, and collaborate effectively. This includes technical training on CI/CD pipelines, containerization, and cloud infrastructure, as well as soft skills training on collaboration and communication.
4. **Celebrate Wins and Learn from Failures**: As teams adopt DevOps practices, it's important to celebrate successes, whether it's a faster deployment, fewer production issues, or improved collaboration between teams. Recognizing and rewarding these wins helps build momentum and encourages other teams to adopt DevOps. At the same time, failures should be viewed as learning opportunities rather than setbacks. Conducting blameless post-mortems allows teams to reflect on what went wrong, learn from mistakes, and improve future processes.

Automation Challenges: Balancing Speed and Control

While automation is one of the cornerstones of DevOps, it can also introduce challenges, especially for organizations that are used to manual processes. Automating the testing, deployment, and monitoring of applications requires a careful balance between speed and control. Teams may be concerned that automating processes will result in loss of visibility or control over production environments.

Overcoming Automation Challenges

1. **Automate Gradually**: Automation doesn't need to happen all at once. Start by automating the most repetitive and time-consuming tasks, such as unit testing or infrastructure provisioning. As teams become more comfortable with automation, more complex processes like continuous delivery and security checks can be automated. This incremental approach helps teams maintain control and confidence in the system.
2. **Build-in Safety Nets**: One of the concerns with automation is that it may introduce errors or cause disruptions if not properly managed. To address this, organizations should build safety nets into their automation processes. This could include implementing automated testing, using canary releases to test new features on a small group of users before a full rollout, or automating rollbacks in case of failure. These safety nets provide teams with the confidence to move quickly without sacrificing stability.
3. **Create Clear Governance Policies**: Automation should be governed by clear policies and procedures that define how and when code can be deployed to production. For example, organizations might require that all code passes a series of automated tests before it can be deployed or mandate that certain security checks are performed before each release. Clear governance ensures that automation is used responsibly and aligns with business objectives.

Measuring Success: Demonstrating the Value of DevOps

One of the key challenges when transitioning to DevOps is measuring success. Without clear metrics, it can be difficult to demonstrate the value of DevOps to stakeholders and justify continued investment in the transformation. Organizations must define and track key performance indicators (KPIs) that reflect the success of their DevOps initiatives.

Overcoming Measurement Challenges

1. **Define Meaningful KPIs**: The success of DevOps should be measured using metrics that align with business goals. Some common DevOps KPIs include:

    - Deployment Frequency: How often new code is deployed to production.
    - Lead Time for Changes: The time it takes to go from code commit to production.
    - Change Failure Rate: The percentage of deployments that result in production failures.
    - Mean Time to Recovery (MTTR): The average time it takes to recover from a failure in production.

    These KPIs provide a clear picture of how DevOps is improving the speed, quality, and reliability of software delivery.

2. **Track Both Technical and Business Metrics**: In addition to technical KPIs, it's important to track business metrics that demonstrate the impact of DevOps on overall business outcomes. This could include metrics such as customer satisfaction, revenue growth, or market share. By tying DevOps success to business results, it becomes easier to justify continued investment and expansion of DevOps practices.
3. **Use Dashboards for Visibility**: Visualizing key metrics through dashboards can help teams and stakeholders track progress and identify areas for improvement. Tools like Grafana, Datadog, or Jenkins can be used to create

real-time dashboards that display the health of the pipeline, performance metrics, and error rates. Providing visibility into the entire DevOps process helps build trust and ensures that everyone is aligned on objectives.

Summary

In this chapter we have explored how transitioning from a traditional IT environment to a DevOps approach is not without its challenges. Silos, legacy systems, resistance to change, and concerns about automation can all create roadblocks. However, by promoting collaboration, modernizing incrementally, automating responsibly, and tracking meaningful metrics, organizations can overcome these challenges and successfully implement DevOps.

As we've looked at in this chapter, implementing DevOps requires more than just adopting new tools—it requires cultural change, process improvements, and a willingness to embrace new ways of working. With the right strategy, organizations can realize the full benefits of DevOps, including faster time to market, improved software quality, and enhanced operational efficiency.

In the next chapter, we will explore how to measure the success of a DevOps implementation in more detail, focusing on key metrics and KPIs that provide insight into performance, reliability, and overall business impact. This will help organizations assess their DevOps journey and continuously improve their processes.

7
MEASURING SUCCESS: KEY METRICS AND KPIS FOR DEVOPS PERFORMANCE

One of the biggest challenges organizations face when implementing DevOps is knowing how to measure success. Without clear, objective metrics, it can be difficult to assess whether the DevOps transformation is delivering the expected benefits or to identify areas for improvement. In this chapter, we will explore the key performance indicators (KPIs) and metrics that can be used to measure the success of a DevOps implementation. By tracking the right metrics, organizations can ensure that they are achieving the desired outcomes, such as faster delivery, improved quality, and greater operational efficiency.

Why Measuring DevOps Success Matters

DevOps success is often defined by more than just technical achievements. It's about delivering business value by improving the speed and quality of software delivery while maintaining or even enhancing stability and security. Measuring success allows organizations to:

1. **Demonstrate Business Impact**: DevOps initiatives should ultimately contribute to broader business goals, such as increased customer satisfaction, revenue growth, or reduced operational costs. By measuring success, teams can demonstrate how DevOps contributes to these outcomes.
2. **Drive Continuous Improvement**: DevOps is based on the principle of continuous improvement. By tracking metrics over time, teams can identify bottlenecks, inefficiencies, and areas for improvement. This ensures that processes are constantly evolving and improving.
3. **Align Teams Around Shared Goals**: Metrics provide a common language for development, operations, and business teams. By focusing on shared KPIs, teams can align their efforts and work collaboratively toward common goals.

Key DevOps Metrics to Track

There are several important metrics that organizations can use to measure the success of their DevOps initiatives. These metrics cover different aspects of the software delivery lifecycle, from deployment frequency to system reliability and recovery time.

1. Deployment Frequency

Deployment frequency measures how often new code is successfully deployed to production. This is a key indicator of the speed and efficiency of the development pipeline. In traditional IT models, deployments may occur infrequently—perhaps once a month or even less often—due to the complexity and risk involved. DevOps, on the other hand, aims to increase deployment frequency, allowing teams to release features and fixes more frequently.

- Why It Matters: Frequent deployments are a sign that the development and operations teams are working together effectively, that automation is in place, and that the pipeline is running smoothly. Frequent deployments also mean that teams can respond quickly to changes in customer needs or market conditions.
- Benchmark: High-performing DevOps teams may deploy to production multiple times per day, while lower-performing teams may deploy only once per month or less.

2. Lead Time for Changes

Lead time for changes measures the time it takes from when a developer commits code to when that code is successfully deployed in production. This metric reflects the efficiency of the CI/CD pipeline and the team's ability to deliver new features and fixes quickly.

- Why It Matters: Shorter lead times indicate that teams can deliver value to customers and the business more quickly. It also means that problems are detected and resolved earlier in the process, reducing the risk of issues reaching production.
- Benchmark: High-performing DevOps teams typically have a lead time of less than one hour, while lower-performing teams may have lead times of several weeks or more.

3. Change Failure Rate

The change failure rate measures the percentage of deployments that result in a failure, such as a system outage, performance degradation, or a rollback. This metric reflects the quality of the changes being deployed and the stability of the deployment process.

- Why It Matters: A high change failure rate indicates that there are issues in the testing, validation, or deployment processes. It suggests that deployments are not adequately tested, that teams are moving too quickly without proper safeguards, or that there are problems with the underlying infrastructure.
- Benchmark: High-performing teams typically have a change failure rate of less than 15%, meaning that the vast majority of their deployments are successful. Lower-performing teams may have failure rates above 50%.

4. Mean Time to Recovery (MTTR)

Mean time to recovery (MTTR) measures how long it takes to restore service after a production failure. This metric reflects the team's ability to respond quickly to incidents and resolve issues in production.

- Why It Matters: A lower MTTR indicates that the team can quickly diagnose and resolve issues, minimizing the impact on customers and the business. This is particularly important for organizations that rely on continuous availability of their services, such as e-commerce platforms, financial services, health services and those serving vulnerable people.
- Benchmark: High-performing teams typically have an MTTR of less than one hour, meaning that they can restore service quickly after an incident. Lower-performing teams may take several hours or even days to recover from failures.

5. Automation Coverage

Automation coverage measures the percentage of the software delivery lifecycle that is automated. This includes tasks such as building, testing, deployment, and infrastructure provisioning. The goal of DevOps is to automate as much of the delivery process as possible to reduce manual effort, increase consistency, and minimize the risk of human error.

- Why It Matters: High automation coverage ensures that the team can deliver software quickly and reliably. It also frees up time for teams to focus on more strategic activities, such as innovation and problem-solving, rather than manual tasks.
- Benchmark: High-performing DevOps teams typically aim for 80% to 90% automation coverage, with the remaining manual steps reserved for tasks that require human judgment, such as final quality checks or approvals.

6. Infrastructure as Code (IaC) Adoption

Infrastructure as Code (IaC) refers to the practice of managing infrastructure (such as servers, networks, and databases) using code. IaC allows teams to automate the provisioning, configuration, and scaling of infrastructure, ensuring consistency across environments and reducing the risk of configuration drift.

- Why It Matters: Adopting IaC improves the scalability and reliability of infrastructure, reduces manual configuration errors, and enables faster, more consistent deployments. IaC is also critical for supporting cloud-based and containerized environments, where infrastructure needs to be dynamically provisioned and managed.
- Benchmark: High-performing teams should aim for near-total adoption of IaC for managing their infrastructure, ensuring that all environments are defined and managed through code.

7. Customer Satisfaction

While technical metrics are essential for tracking DevOps success, it's also important to measure the impact on customers and business outcomes. Customer satisfaction metrics, such as Net Promoter Score (NPS), customer retention rates, or feedback from user surveys, provide insight into how well DevOps practices are delivering value to end users.

- Why It Matters: Ultimately, the goal of DevOps is to deliver better products and services to customers and the business more quickly. If DevOps is working, customer satisfaction should improve as new features are delivered more rapidly, bugs are fixed more quickly, and the overall user experience becomes more reliable.
- Benchmark: The target for customer satisfaction will vary depending on the industry and customer base. However, organizations should aim to see an upward trend in satisfaction scores following the implementation of DevOps.

Visualizing Metrics: The Power of Dashboards

One of the most effective ways to track and communicate DevOps performance is by using dashboards. Dashboards provide real-time visibility into the key metrics that matter most to your organization. By visualizing metrics on a dashboard, teams can quickly identify trends, spot bottlenecks, and make data-driven decisions.

Popular tools for creating DevOps dashboards include:

- **Grafana**: Grafana is an open-source platform for monitoring and observability. It integrates with a wide variety of data sources and allows teams to create highly customizable dashboards for tracking metrics such as deployment frequency, error rates, and system performance.
- **Datadog**: Datadog provides comprehensive monitoring and analytics for applications, infrastructure, and logs. It offers out-of-the-box dashboards for tracking DevOps metrics and integrates with popular tools like AWS, Kubernetes, and Docker.
- **Jenkins Dashboards**: Jenkins, a popular CI/CD tool, offers built-in dashboards for tracking the health of the CI/CD pipeline, including build times, test results, and deployment status.

By creating dashboards that display key metrics in real time, teams can quickly respond to issues, identify areas for improvement, and demonstrate the impact of their DevOps practices to stakeholders.

Aligning Metrics with Business Goals

While technical metrics provide valuable insights into the performance of the DevOps pipeline, it's important to ensure that these metrics are aligned with broader business goals. For example, faster deployments and lower failure rates should ultimately lead to increased revenue, reduced operational costs, improved customer satisfaction or more citizens served faster. By aligning DevOps metrics with business outcomes, organizations can demonstrate the real value of DevOps to leadership and stakeholders.

Key business-aligned metrics include:

- Time to Market: How quickly the organization can deliver new products or features to market.
- Operational Efficiency: The reduction in manual effort or operational overhead as a result of automation and improved collaboration.
- Cost Savings: The cost savings achieved through faster recovery times, reduced downtime, and more efficient use of infrastructure.

Summary

Measuring the success of DevOps is an ongoing process. By tracking key metrics such as deployment frequency, lead time, change failure rate, and mean time to recovery, organizations can continuously assess their performance and identify areas for improvement. Visualizing these metrics through dashboards and aligning them with business goals ensures that DevOps initiatives deliver real value to the organization.

In the next chapter, we'll look to the future of IT operations and explore how organizations can scale DevOps practices across the enterprise, addressing governance, compliance, and other challenges that arise as DevOps matures.

8
THE FUTURE OF I.T. OPERATIONS: SCALING DEVOPS FOR ENTERPRISE GROWTH

As organizations experience the benefits of DevOps—faster delivery times, improved product quality, and increased operational efficiency—they often look for ways to scale these practices across the enterprise. However, scaling DevOps is not simply about applying the same processes and tools to a larger number of teams or projects. It requires a thoughtful approach to governance, compliance, security, and cross-team collaboration. In this final chapter, we will explore how organizations can successfully scale DevOps, address common challenges, and maintain agility as they grow.

The Challenges of Scaling DevOps

Scaling DevOps across an enterprise presents unique challenges that may not be as apparent when DevOps is implemented on a smaller scale. As the number of teams and projects grows, so does the complexity of managing and coordinating them. Common challenges include:

1. **Maintaining Consistency Across Teams** As multiple teams adopt DevOps practices, it can be difficult to maintain consistency in processes, tools, and workflows. Different teams may choose different tools for automation, testing, and deployment, which can lead to fragmented systems and a lack of standardization.
2. **Governance and Compliance** Large organizations often have strict governance and compliance requirements, particularly in highly regulated industries such as finance or healthcare. As DevOps practices are scaled, it's important to ensure that teams adhere to regulatory requirements, security policies, and corporate governance standards without sacrificing agility. Governance must be effective but minimise delivery friction.
3. **Security at Scale** As more teams adopt DevOps practices and the pace of delivery accelerates, it becomes increasingly important to integrate security into every stage of the development and deployment pipeline.

Security risks can multiply as the volume of code, infrastructure, and dependencies grows, making it essential to adopt practices like DevSecOps.
4. **Cross-Team Collaboration** In a large organization, multiple teams often work on different parts of the same product or service. Without effective coordination, this can lead to siloed efforts, duplicated work, and misaligned priorities. Ensuring that all teams are aligned and collaborating effectively is a major challenge when scaling DevOps.

Best Practices for Scaling DevOps

To successfully scale DevOps, organizations need to adopt strategies that promote consistency, governance, security, and collaboration across teams while maintaining the agility and flexibility that DevOps enables.

1. Standardize Processes and Tools

While DevOps encourages teams to be autonomous and make decisions that best fit their workflows, some level of standardization is necessary when scaling. Standardizing key processes and tools across teams ensures that everyone is aligned, reduces fragmentation, and makes it easier to manage the entire development pipeline.

- Tool Standardization: Encourage the adoption of a common set of tools for CI/CD, testing, monitoring, and security across teams. This can include tools like Jenkins, GitLab, Kubernetes, Terraform, and Prometheus. Standardization also makes it easier to onboard new teams and maintain consistent performance metrics.
- Process Standardization: Define standard processes for critical stages of the DevOps lifecycle, such as code review, automated testing, security scans, and incident response. By establishing these practices as

organizational norms, you ensure that all teams are following best practices and minimizing risks.

2. Adopt a Platform Engineering Approach

As organizations scale, managing infrastructure for multiple teams becomes more complex. A platform engineering approach can help address this challenge. Platform engineering involves creating a shared infrastructure platform that teams can use to build, test, and deploy their applications. This platform includes standardized tools, automation frameworks, and self-service capabilities, allowing development teams to focus on coding rather than managing infrastructure.

- Self-Service Capabilities: By providing development teams with self-service tools to provision infrastructure, deploy applications, and run tests, you reduce dependencies on centralized operations teams and enable faster delivery.
- Platform as a Product: Treat the shared platform as a product with its own development team. Continuously improve the platform based on feedback from users (i.e., the development teams), and ensure it evolves to meet the needs of the growing organization.

3. Integrate Security with DevSecOps

As organizations scale DevOps, integrating security into every stage of the software delivery process becomes crucial. This approach is known as DevSecOps—combining development, security, and operations to ensure that security is "baked in" rather than being an afterthought.

- Automated Security Testing: Incorporate automated security testing into the CI/CD pipeline. Tools like Snyk, Aqua Security, and Twistlock can scan code, containers, and dependencies for vulnerabilities, ensuring that security issues are identified early in the process.

- Shift Left: In DevSecOps, security practices are "shifted left," meaning they are applied earlier in the development process. This involves conducting security checks during the coding, testing, and build stages rather than waiting until deployment.
- Security as Code: Use Infrastructure as Code (IaC) to enforce security policies and ensure that infrastructure is configured securely. For example, you can use tools like Terraform to define security groups, firewall rules, and access controls in code, making security policies consistent and repeatable.

4. **Implement Governance and Compliance Frameworks**

Large organizations often have strict governance and compliance requirements that must be adhered to, even as DevOps practices are scaled. Implementing a governance framework ensures that teams can move quickly without compromising on compliance.

- Automated Compliance Checks: Use automated tools to enforce compliance with regulatory and governance standards. Tools like HashiCorp Sentinel, Open Policy Agent (OPA), and AWS Config can automatically check that infrastructure, applications, and processes comply with predefined policies.
- Audit Trails: Ensure that all changes to code, infrastructure, and configurations are tracked in version control. This provides a clear audit trail for regulatory compliance and allows teams to quickly identify the source of any issues.
- Continuous Compliance: Rather than conducting compliance reviews at the end of a project, adopt continuous compliance practices by integrating compliance checks into the CI/CD pipeline. This allows teams to identify and resolve compliance issues early in the process.

5. Foster a Culture of Continuous Learning and Improvement

As organizations scale, it's important to maintain the DevOps culture of continuous learning and improvement. Encouraging teams to experiment, learn from their failures, and iterate on their processes ensures that DevOps practices remain effective as the organization grows.

- Blameless Post-Mortems: When failures or incidents occur, conduct blameless post-mortems to analyze what went wrong and how it can be prevented in the future. This fosters a culture of learning rather than blame and encourages teams to take ownership of their mistakes.
- Knowledge Sharing: Create opportunities for teams to share their learnings and best practices across the organization. This can be done through internal conferences, knowledge-sharing sessions, or documentation that is accessible to all teams.
- Experimentation and Innovation: Encourage teams to experiment with new tools, technologies, and processes. By fostering a culture of innovation, organizations can continuously improve their DevOps practices and stay ahead of industry trends.

6. Measure and Optimize Performance

As DevOps scales, it's important to continuously measure performance and optimize processes across teams. Tracking the right metrics ensures that teams remain aligned with business goals and can identify areas for improvement.

- Cross-Team Metrics: As discussed in the previous chapter, tracking metrics such as deployment frequency, lead time, change failure rate, and mean time to recovery (MTTR) provides valuable insights into the performance of each team. By comparing these metrics across teams,

organizations can identify best practices and areas where improvements are needed.
- Business Impact Metrics: In addition to technical metrics, it's important to track metrics that reflect the broader business impact of DevOps. These can include customer satisfaction, revenue growth, and operational cost savings. Aligning DevOps metrics with business goals ensures that the DevOps transformation is delivering tangible value to the organization.

The Role of Leadership in Scaling DevOps

Leadership plays a crucial role in scaling DevOps across the enterprise. Leaders must set the vision for DevOps, provide the necessary resources and support, and remove barriers that hinder progress. As DevOps practices scale, leadership must also focus on maintaining the right culture—one that prioritizes collaboration, innovation, and continuous improvement.

- Vision and Strategy: Leaders must clearly communicate the organization's DevOps vision and strategy. This includes defining the business goals that DevOps is expected to achieve and aligning teams around those goals.
- Invest in People and Training: Scaling DevOps requires continuous investment in people. Leaders should provide training and development opportunities to help teams improve their skills in automation, security, and cloud infrastructure.
- Empower Teams: Leadership must empower teams to take ownership of their work and make decisions. This means giving teams the autonomy to choose the tools and processes that work best for them, while ensuring alignment with organizational goals.

Summary

> The future of DevOps is bright. As organizations continue to adopt and scale DevOps practices, they will unlock new levels of agility, innovation, and efficiency. However, scaling DevOps is not without its challenges. It requires careful planning, thoughtful governance, and a commitment to maintaining the right culture.
>
> The culture change is key, if that cannot be mastered then the process will probably not succeed. I have worked in many environments that today one would call toxic, where staff were fearful to speak up, got blamed and would rarely make decisions for fear of reprisals. I make it my mission to change these types of environments. Staff must not only be empowered to be autonomous, but they <u>must feel</u> empowered and be autonomous.
>
> By standardizing processes, adopting platform engineering, integrating security, and fostering continuous learning, organizations can successfully scale DevOps across the enterprise. As DevOps practices evolve, organizations will be well-positioned to respond to changing market demands, deliver better products to customers, and drive business growth.

As I conclude, remember that DevOps is not a one-time initiative—it is an ongoing journey. As technology and business needs evolve, so too will DevOps practices. By staying committed to continuous improvement, collaboration, and innovation, your organization can thrive in an increasingly digital world.

Whether you need to adopt new technology or you have a drive for digital transformation, the use of DevOps, and with it Agile methods, any organization can achieve their goals.

ABOUT THE AUTHOR

Mark Davies is a husband and father of four children who has been working in all aspects of technology for over 30 years. Having worked his way through all areas in IT from programming, networks, security, operations, project delivery he has, for the last 15 years been operating as a consultant and interim IT Director and CIO for Public and Private sector clients through his own private practice.
He has worked for corporate clients such as IBM, HP, Boeing, Marks & Spencer, Sainsbury's and many UK public sector clients including councils and healthcare providers.

If you would like to get in touch, then please reach him on email: mark@alcedinconsulting.com

www.ingramcontent.com/pod-product-compliance
Lightning Source LLC
Chambersburg PA
CBHW070409230526
45471CB00006B/2721